This book is dedicated to my family:
Kathy, Sean, Sile, Caitriona and Eamonn

ACKNOWLEDGEMENTS

The author acknowledges publication of these poems in
the magazines Cyphers , Acorn (Dublin Writers' Workshop),
Poetry Ireland Review, Burren Meitheal,
The Secondary Teacher, The Other Clare and Voicefree
Broadsheet. Acknowledgement also to the 'New Irish
Writing' page in the (now defunct) Irish Press, to the
'Writing in the West' page in the Connaught Tribune and
to the poetry anthology 'Nineties Poetry ' (UK).

CONTENTS

DISPATCHES *from the New Settlements*

RECOLLECTIONS *of the Old Country*

DISPATCHES
from the New Settlements ...

EARLY DISPATCHES

Scarce into our second week we find
long caterpillar tracks when we return
at evening. Just today another cable
swings in long U-shapes against the sky
and poppies wave on mounds of broken soil.

The road is stopped at stunted hedges gathering
strength to tackle scutch and briar and thistle.
All that once was green is grey here now
and dust hangs in the air as metal monsters
masticate the hillsides, delve ravines.

We make our meals on one small camping stove,
and talk about the mortgage. Only just last night
we heard the water gurgle in the taps
at last. Tonight we thought we saw a light
shine two doors down. Have we neighbours?

SUBURBAN BEDROOM SONNET:
MORNING POURS GOD'S PLENTY

Morning pours God's plenty: java sparrows
perch on plum trees, thrust their breasts out, fill
their picture frame with song. Doorknobs blaze
effulgent, clothes on chairs disclose their folds,
shoes coalesce and share a shadow,
buttons glow. An open book allows
a single page stands upright, wave, recall
that last monastic moment before sleep.

Nine hundred million miles and more across
the sterile void this waterfall of liquid
fire has plunged a headlong torrent, crashed
through fields of asteroids and stirred the storms
of Venus, eternally ordained to slant
this golden scripture on this bedroom wall.

ROADWORKER
(for Martin Monaghen)

No suburban handkerchief
of grass and verge and veg.
is daily so well tended as
the mile of road that threads
from Lucan Bridge and Shackleton's
past CPI up Tinker's Hill
and on through ambuscade of hedge
and bower to Luttrelstown back gate.

Morning peers across the walls
of concrete block on block —
A million single stiffened spikes
shine blue and grey beneath the frost:
the thaw begins — But hours ago
the watery sun and gravel swung
in crescents from his spade and caught
the frozen reaches of his road.

Rattle out the lawnmower now —
Time to spike the soil,
battle against thistle, nettle, dock,
dandelion and blacktop, oil
the shears. Already he has started
(his coat a yellow warning splash!)
to hack and trim and sweep his mile
of bramble, briar and honeysuckle stem.

Caught in chimney stacks, the sun
is stumbling over roof-edge,
struggling torn down pebbledash,
spilling jewels on window ledge:
up Tandy's Lane towards Dodsboro
he comes with sloping spade, with gold
of evening on the blade, a bag
of groceries dangling from his hand.

VOYAGER

Photopolarimeter,
gravitational assist are
words that warp the airwaves, scatter
unofficial strikes and interest
rates in slipstream, agitate
a drift of early morning tidings
out beyond the undersides
of Saturn's multicoloured rings.

Grey waters surge down Lucan weir
to prove our laws of physics, dying
leaves reveal all chemistry
in colour. Bus-queue courtesies
conceal our inner galaxies
where each will sail his caravel, scan
peaks and troughs, evaluate
primordial bombardments.

Throughout this day your silver shell
will break across the lowering skies,
skim fast atop October trees,
score corridors through sulphurous clouds —
Across my mind quick syllables
vibrate, create wide-angled views,
computerised trajectories

of Enceladus, Iapetus -
of Phoebe (fickle satellite)
and many other unknown moons
propelled through scarlet stratospheres
above the sandstormed cratered plains
where equatorial winds scream out
their several thousand miles per hour...

SUBURBAN SPRING

The waste spaces green again
and rooks pebble-step on vacant sites
and hibernators hesitate, emerge:
window-cleaners, FOR SALE signs, double-
glazing salesmen, boys who'll cut your grass
for fifty pence break a season's cover.

Hemmed by kerb and paving, jaded stalks
stem upwards, roadside saplings strain
supports and shirted men spend weekends
delving small enclosures, counting seeds
from sachets into careful rills. Children,
(one foot taller) test new bikes.

Easter eggs fill up the shelves
and indoor games are beaten back
by beach balls, plastic buckets, package
holiday brochures. Each evening
God's own engineers work nixers
on the backdrops, key in extra lights.

And now the night is like a blade's
chill cutting slash along the wrists, and winter
loiters down dark lanes and kicks at clumps
of withered Christmas trees thrown in behind
back walls. He spits, unclasps his aerosol
and scrawls a message: I'LL BE BACK.

ENCLOSURES

Concrete blocks are stacked along
the footpaths: giants jigsaws waiting
for the Long Weekend assembly
into boundary walls, coal bunkers.

Piles of sand and gravel fill up
driveways, and neighbours plan together
how to shut out daylight, dam
the morning gold that washes grass.

Stung to scorn he structures out
a palisade of pointed stakes
and nails to every whitened board
his pride in the particular.

And any weary traveller
who charts an urban odyssey
of numbered doors and angled roads,
of crescents, courts and drives and groves

will shout aloud and point beyond
the mounting waves and waves of grey
stone walls to where white shafts rise up
excalibur-like against the sky.

URBAN GUERRILLA
(Polygonaceae, Rumex Crispus. comm. 'Curled Dock')

All despite the poison gun
the wicked seed endures. Despite
the killer spray, the razored hoe,
the rhetoric — All winter long
she hides, unwinds her coils, lays down
her secret network in the clay.

And Spring is come and sap is sucked
alive again: no-warning stems
explode between the nursery shoots —
Each night her glabrous leaves caress
herbaceous borders, pick soft targets,
withdraw at dawn with reddened edges.

Enemy implacable
of geometric paths and gnomes
she shakes contagion on the winds,
abhors the vapid symmetry
of alien imposed plantation:
not her province garrisoned lawns.

Rabid slut of botany,
whorl-whore of bloodied green
her calyx lifts where desolate
and dispossessed must share out scree
and scutch with nettle, burnt -out car —
Every purge she'll suffer. She'll survive.

And Autumn comes and once again
eradication programmes: *This,
the scourge and cancer of our times
must, nay will, be destroyed!*
The wicked seed in winter quarters,
binds her wounds and bides her time.

CAMPAIGN
(for Michael and Anne Finnegan)

Cum esset Caesar in citeriore Gallia in hibernis ... crebri ad
eum rumores afferebantur, litterisque item Labieni certior
fiebat omnes Belgas ... contra populum Romanum coniurare...
De Bello Gallico II.

(When Caesar was in hither Gaul, in winter quarters ... frequent
rumours were brought to him and furthermore he was
informed by the letters of Labienus that the Belgians were
conspiring against Rome... The Gallic Wars, Book 2)

Bristling out with slogans, manifestos —
stabbing out the selling points, keylines
double-blocked in heavy type (two-colour
letterbox-sized) — Yet, he is withal
not proof against the purple clouds, his collar
not a match for thunder and the sudden
ambuscade of sleet that speckles pavements,
shatters converse, congregates the faithful
in bus-shelters, cigarette smoke mixing
with indelible city-smell of wet cement.

All huddled in a doorway, dog-eared leaflets
at the ready, broken wads of wet
electoral registers wedged underarm,
he draws his canvas tight across the well-known
strongholds, sends forays down sympathetic
roads, attempts to sandwich socialism
with local bread-and-butter issues, skewers
the body politic on two or three
sharp sentences he hopes won't sound mere nonsense
to the housewife standing hoover-horn in hand.

Here, where several streets collide, and loafers
lie along the walls like algae, dogs
smell cracks in lampposts, plastic supermarket
bags go swirling in eternal circles —
He it is ignores the catcalls, jeers
and, foot upon the threshold, argues for
a better world, equality and justice —
pausing only when he sees a stain
of blood appear on several leaflets, finds
the razor page has stigmatised his palms.

Alone at last atop a bus (no straining
smile, no lapel-stickers, party badge)
he reads a better poet who pens a bitter
line or two about the politician's
art of treachery — Tears of betrayal
well in his eyes, ascetic January branches
clatter on the bus-roof — Stay up high within
your lofty towers, ye rhyming schemers: here
is one prepared to send his soul out steaming

wrapped in yesterday's evening papers (NOW
NINE HUNDRED THOUSAND SEEK AMERICAN VISAS)
to be passed from hand to hand, consumed when pubs
shut down and darkness gropes democracy
in corners and the Late News summarises
still one more opinion poll and sleep
recalls the Latin prose of Caesar, wind-
whipped tent in hither Gaul, in winter quarters,
trestle-table strewn with close reports
from Labienus auguring a long campaign.

DEMONSTRATIONS OF AFFECTION

Will these workmen never learn the careful
grudging discourse of the city? Several
months awork along this major artery
to pump another hundred thousand bodies
daily tight-lipped into town — Several

months of cable-laying, paralleling
sewage channels, flinging bridges over
minor roads and still their salutations
not yet ground to single particles? — No?
The half smile and the face averted? — No?

These broad windbeaten faces topped
with wild sunquifted shocks of greybrown hair
are clearly exponential of wide skies
beyond our concourse, open fields
where there was time to share the word of friendship

full in all its syllables — Where hand
could handclasp hand and all the lexicon
of neighboured language flow from palm to palm.
Like sailors come to port in some strange land
with little knowledge of the local tongue,

how can they come to terms with this, our clipped
suburban dialect bred of distance and unease
and close desire for anonymity? —
Like sailors come to port they wander through
our mute bazaars, their proffered coin of converse

unacceptable. But safe against
seduction always they who demonstrate
affection, they who tender love in face
of flat denial, who spurn the byroads,
build the highway straight in towards the heart.

SNOW QUEEN

Splinters in my heart her eyes this morning
when she picked her way across the dark
Jurassic mass of Lucan's half-completed
By-Pass, shoes so white against the turmoil
of the clay, her stole so tightly drawn
across her shoulders, neck laid bare to frosts

And early shoppers shielded eyes, and workmen —
frozen in the act of splitting shale-rock
wide apart — dared no whistle, jibe,
no risqué remark, but stood instead enchanted.
All who saw her walk the supermarket
tarmac past delivery vans, unloading

lorries — All who saw her debutante's
ball-gown skim inches above ground
were blinded: housewives momentarily
awaiting once again the foot would first
the threshold, children staring gape-eyed
at the Snow Queen come from bedtime story

fresh from northern midnight wastes of whiteness,
hint of glacial fragrance in her wake.
Then it was I felt the meltdown
in my soul for you, Snow Queen,
and for your hurried step so far
from distant longitudes that stretch so far up towards

the polar cap, Andromeda, Aurora
Borealis, and the narrow gap
so few have ever entered, ever heard
the splendid music of the spheres. For you
can shape the jagged ice to words like faith
and hope — Your silver-painted fingernails

unfaltering — While all I have are fragments
stored a lifetime in my heart despite
all disappointments, adverse trades. Tonight,
when once again I try to fit together
all my broken bits of glass with words,
your certain stride, your flowing scarf start up

a trembling in my hand. I find your sideways
glance has cracked the prism of my mind
and set my fragments spinning. What can pen
impart to match the imprint that your heel
this morning made across my half-completed
path of eighty years? I see you turn

into suburban streets. I see you walk
past endless rows of gates, low garden walls
your stain of whiteness fading out of sight
and all your frailty trailing out behind you.
Quick, Snow Queen, before the thaw comes —
Fast, before the rains, before the marrow

weakens and the back bends, before
the brittle teethe become uncertain and the jowl
drags down the jaw — Like splinters in my heart
your eyes this morning when the upturned sods
and vampire frosts conspired to cross our paths —
Fast, Snow Queen, and compass out a course

due north where whiteness pains the eye and sun
denies the dark for days — where stainless lakes
reflect the stars, and fragments spell at last
the soul's harsh compromise with life:
all that flesh is heir to , yes — But strength
enough for all endurance too, and love.

ATLANTIS

This my wheel a prow to part
the roadside pools — this galleon's bow
will skirt a cape, will plough these Bering Straits
stretched out Mercator-like before me.

Waters wash behind: high branches
vein the shining seas again
with shipping lanes. Busily I employ
my charts and compass — morning moves

(my midshipman) commanding decks
cleared, hatches opened. India lies ahead
and then all Asia hoves in view,
all endless tracts of blue. My orders

reach the dwindling stores below:
Break out a case or two of hope! —
for joy swells in my throat and now,
Magellan, I can tell it's time

to risk again the hell of scurvy,
high-sea piracy, bad storms,
betrayal — can tell again it's time
to risk all adverse trades arising

out of kindness, time to square
the shoulders, face into the rain
and (heart, oh heart!) again essay
the shrouded mountain ranges of Atlantis.

JANUARY AND HOW TO HOLD HER
(at Collins' Bridge, The Royal Canal, January)

One of those old masters who delights
in scrawny hedges and ploughed fields
was out this morning with his sketch-block,

stripped this narrow bridge to its essentials
leaving just enough to launch the eye
across long broken strokes that mark

where blade cut into clay. Then pencil points
betokening early birds, scuffed grey
on grey for clouds and mountains and then later

when he stood before the easel, head down,
straining back for January and how
to hold her — Pulled a stool up close and took

a tiny brush and pinched the sable tip
between his thumb and finger, draped a lace
of snow across the mountains and , for those

must eke their lives out on the margins
of the canvas, carefully touched the bridge
with one or two stick figures. Delicately.

THE ORANGE BUS
(from a child's drawing)

The orange bus (with blue and yellow
zigzag stripes) is hurtling sideways
towards the city, driver huge
behind his quite enormous wheel,
all other windows blank. And here

we are arrived at last and cars
are stacked on top of one another
but the orange bus (stripes lost
en route and driver too) has skidded
to a halt atop the bladed railings.

Everyone gets off (although
a head or two gets left behind).
Inside the Natural Museum stick
figures view mysterious shapes,
thin arms shoot upwards in surprise.

And colour everywhere (except
a door marked EXIT: black and white).
A Somethingsaurus rears its neck,
its bones a set of careful strokes,
its tail extending twice its length —

Ferocious, yet it manages
a half smile, looks like it might like
a walk, a biscuit, or at the very
least a friendly rub along
its several-million-years-old nose.

The Gallery next, and not much colour
here. A group of careless smudges
stand around a picture of a man
who twirls moustaches, holds a sword
and smiles (but grimly and unlike

our bony friend) and looks as if
he'd like to cut off any heads
not safely left aboard the orange bus.
More prominent than the paintings one
large red fire extinguisher.

It's eating-time at last: a bigger stick
in flowery dress dispenses packages:
There are picnic tables but the grass
is best — So very green, the egg-shaped sun
so high and bright. And still to come

the trip home sideways in the orange bus.

POEM
for Eamonn

My threeyearold and me
we kick the ball across the green
erratically.
Now fastforward, now
fastdoubling backward, now
diagonally.

I am Eusebio, he
Diego Maradona, we
together make a team
unbeatable this morning
on the green.

Formidable, our volleys
deadly accurate, half-chances
taken swiftly, neatly curling
shots inside the posts
that train young saplings.

At the kerb we pause: he
all eager forward. I
look back along our path:
a straggled line of ruffled grass
fast fading. Fading
far too fast.

WHEN WE GO TO BED

When we go to bed we pause a step
along the stairway, say goodnight because
we hope the night will fare us into goodness
only and because we sense all sleep's
an endless and slow circling in the space
between two capitals — the one so full
of wakenings-up in small untidy rooms —
the other where we must embrace our fears:

derricks and tower-blocks tensed
straight on the horizon, jagged shapes
that slit the darkness spilling memories
of wrong, the dead we live with daily telling
once again their gain and loss and ours,
the living in strange forms, and then
the centrifugal pull that turns us down
to roads lit up like runways far below

and we begin again the slow descent between
tall buildings, passing once again
that window and the foetal figure naked
on white sheets and feel the ventricles
close off and hear the combination click
behind the heart that shuts down breathing

but this one more time clicks twice. Daylight
roars against the aerilons: good morning.

OUR NEW NEIGHBOUR

That first time he settled in for good
we found it hard to think that any house
like ours would interest him. Preoccupied
with birth and growth and clothes too suddenly

become too small, our minds had never dwelt
for long on fate — we'd viewed the future always
as an open door, a gate that swings
forever outwards into endless fields.

And yet for those who read the leaves in August
or watch September torture a late rose
or mark October steal across the garden
stalking Autumn to a close, this coming

was expected. Time to time sick child
or visiting elder knew his cold attentions —
These exceptions, standing out against
the tide of tricycles, cut knees and lines

of nappies drying, nonetheless were signs
and auguries. That first time his blade
cut flesh in earnest, skin that showed no taint
of infant plague, no stain of age, it cut

through every one of us and all those tiny
particles of dust his visit laid
along our lips in youth began to taste
again of whispers, silent rooms and scenes

we'd long forgotten, now remembered: words
and phrases used as palisades : how such
an one had 'failed', and how another looked
"so shaken", "went so quickly at the end".

Our new neighbour, just moved in, will live
among us always from now on — Become
as unremarkable as we, be seen
at evening leaning casually against a tree

with shears in hand, his deep-set eyes intent
on plots of grass and plants in rows until
a moment comes he straightens, stroll with purpose
towards a door, his knuckle fisted, bone exposed.

FINISHING

One day I'll finish painting this front door
and it will be the last I'll ever paint it. And
when winter rains and summer suns
have cracked the varnish, faded down the stain

another hand will take a brush and stand
a long uneasy balance on a chair
and angle at those high-up awkward places
and find, behind the rim, the bit I missed.

That last time that I paint this door
will be the last time that I'll ever paint it.
But, ignorant of the clicking reel, I'll stand
and calculate how many years

will need to pass before I need to paint
again. I will not see the modest card appear
pinned up against the breastwork,
carefully written, fluttering in the breeze...

... & RECOLLECTIONS *of the Old Country*

AT THE HOLY WELL
(Teampail a' Deirce, Tubber, Co.Clare)

Pilgrim years have littered
broken statuettes and shattered
bits of rosary-bead in fallen
stone on stone. Soft
summer rain has blanched
the votive notes of hand, drained
blue of Virgin, blood of Sacred Heart
down crevices. A strain
of primal piety endures
in rusted horseshoes, scattered coin.

No mystery mantles readily
my shoulders bowed,
my curious fingers touching
weathered edges of worn stone:
deep down within the bowl
a magic eye of water gleams
when I draw back this screen
of briars — A tiny Iris fires:
defines my face in green
of leaf, on blue of open sky.

Whoever treads this right of way
past nodding nettle, meadowsweet
and angle-thorned weed — Who hacks
through tangled undergrowth
of wicked thistle, tumbled stile
and sunken wall — Who finds
where water oozes of so holy
in this hallowed well will
find an icy stillness
filling in around the soul.

A DAY LIKE THIS: THE EVICTION OF NANCY O'HARA
(at Closh, near Bohola, Co. Mayo c.1890)

A Day like this: white clouds and stabbing rain,
then sudden blue and pools strung out like a broken
necklace along a narrow lane, grass
knee-high along the edges and beyond
the hedge a gable-end of stones. A day
like this the soldiery came out of town
to do their duty, some reluctantly,
but duty must be done, the Queen's writ
run throughout her Kingdom from the plains
of Punjab to these fields of West Mayo.

A day like this you stood and clutched your children
to your skirts and watched your bits of delph
and sticks of furniture disturb the wayside
birdnests, felt the heavy heartsob rise
within you when they tipped the bed out
on the grass and when they blinded in
the windows (where you had watched for him long hours
until the news was brought...). They blinded in
the windows with their rifle-butts, unhinged
the door and pulled the chimney down, all
as prescribed by law and strict procedure.

What consolation was it three nights later
that the hooded men took out the bailiff
from his bed, tied up his wife and daughters,
led him back along this narrow road
to where your cottage lay a moonlit rubble,
and stretched and carded him with implements
provided by their sisters at the mill
who stretch and card the wool each day
until it's broken soft and pliable? It's said
he never walked again. Small consolation

for you, Nancy, caught in history's loom —
Your famished children taken in by neighbours,
neighbours waiting too the soldier's boot
along the gravel. You shared impoverished poverty
until at last the letter from the one
who sailed with thousands, harrowed hell, survived
and sent the passage for the rest. You sailed
the deck and clutched your youngest to your skirts
and left the furze to close around the clutch
of stones, to close the wound until one day,
a day like this, only a scar remains.

WINDSURFER

Windsurfer on the waves
at Ballyalla, you who lean
your body light against
grey clouds — How you take
the strain of gale along
the steering bar, your silhouette
against the wakening stars —
How you bear my soul awash,
away from jagged edges.

Windsurfer skimming tight
the tiny tides of Ballyalla, you
who ride so easily the spray
that spreads gull-winged
against the sky, your shadow
high against the dying day —
Give this last crest your best,
windsurfer, skim the sweeping onslaught,
hold the crashing foams at bay.

THE HAND

Back beyond the road past Inagh
where the bogline rises like a spine
along Mount Callan's back, back

beyond the road to Quilty, balanced
on the edge of Europe, back beyond
bare fields where mist is kissing heath

beware The Hand: dismembered index
to forgotten pasts poised pink
and incorporeal on an obelisk

of stone — Beware the penitential nature
of these gable-ends that ring the square.
Beware a sudden rush of hens and she

who fists the grain so ceremonially
and stares at strangers. Don't stare back — her eyes
will search your soul, reveal flint axe heads,

sculpted bone, a fire and figures hunched
skinclad, faceless yet familiar, hands
outstretched and beckoning you back.

RETURNING SWALLOWS
(for Mary O'Keeffe, Carrowkeal, Crusheen, Co.Clare)

What should I tell the swallows come from Egypt
to my eaves? That they can now no longer
count on reckless hospitality? My
younger neighbours, all grown modern-wise
about house-maintenance and the new emulsion paints

remark how nests besmirch the white facade
of this my house, new renovated. How
so easily one can rid the roof of all these
singing loafers never did a hand's turn
all these years around the place but foul

the sills... Still, all these years to travel
from the Valley of the Kings to County Clare —
to wheel, dive, yearly find the selfsame spot
atop the brick, behind the gutter's kind
projecting rim. And I, grown all these years

much better at divining miracles, can
merely stand out on the lawn at evening
marvelling at their punctuality, their
single-minded industry, their
self-assurance in the scheme of things.

BIRD

No man of science
to know what type
of bird is this I've found
with feet curled up

to heaven (now forever
out of reach) or even
how it came to die,
its jet-black eye fixed

firmly on the clouds —
I listen to the hay
that stands rain-rotting
in the fields again this year

and hear of nature's
prodigality, how
she will often hold
her own creation

in contempt. Else why
such wild munificence
of meadow? Why
such swollen waters

drowning daffodils
at Eastertide? Why
this tiny wing so carefully
designed, this tail

aligned for flight
now cast aside? Not
one to know the name
assigned to you in man's

nomenclature, I stroke
your broken bill and sense,
somewhere behind my heart, the chill
of insignificance.

WHEN GRAVEDIGGERS DIE
(in memory of Thomas Scanlan and Denis McNamara, of Crusheen,
Co. Clare who died July 1987)

The two old men who dug the graves
for all who died around Crusheen
these years and years last week themselves
took to the clay. They, who times

more oftener than other men
had heard the ragged shovel-shot
methodically subtract one other slot
from out the gravelled earth —

They who leaned so nonchalant
along the boundary wall, then mixed
unbidden in among the mourners, joined
the decade, then became all

on a sudden all transformed,
their shovels setting them apart,
their heave and heft mechanically
detaching them from us. When

gravediggers die, there must come
a tremor in the crust of time whereby
the world of stones and trees takes pause:
leaves stop sighing, whitened gable-ends

fixate the sun in stasis
momentarily — When nettles
cease their close embrace of headstones,
all uncertain. They who stayed

behind to flatten out the mound
and then to stake the haft, spit
on their palms, push back their caps,
their pipe-smoke trailing incense upwards,

casually surveying all their handiwork
around them — When gravediggers die
we know the world has shifted in its orbit.
They whose spades these many years

have mapped the limits of our lives
must now themselves stare upwards as the earth
collapses downwards, blotting out
the sun and sky. And we...

When gravediggers die, we
feel the loss of lore, the eye
that navigated more than other men
the wide galactic oceans of decay.

IMAGING CREATION
(at Tullymacken Lake, Co. Clare)

For Sile and Caitriona

Tullymacken wrinkles under wind
and wavelets crack and yes —
This is how the world began
and is beginning always.

Earth and rock and water blend
in elemental spill of bluegreengrey
and shelving edges (where
my children play) coax life

ashore among the reeds. Forever
in the fastness of wild islets
(where my children run) discarded
axeheads cleave the silt, and bone

and stone and shell become
white sand, washed landwards. Yes,
this is how the world began
and is beginning always.

CRAGGED VALLEY

Palpitates the pulse of time
in decorated buckle, crumbling
scroll, gold amulet or

jam-jars spilling spiders,
scattered shards of dresser delph?
Old Quinlan was the last

to hasp this blistered door. No
Royal Tomb, his tumbled house
hoards no jewelled goblets,

ornamented bronze, no
sacred picture-praise of gods
adorns his peeling walls.

A shutter thuds, a hinge sings
in the wind, an iron bed
stands naked and a chair

kneels in a corner. One
small window, fringed around
with broken glass, still frames

the crop of cragged rock that vaults
this valley where, for years on years,
Old Quinlan once was king.

GLORIA MUNDI

This morning after rain I saw
the glory of the world again:

how grey stonewoven walls can stitch
green fields together endlessly;

how metal gates can decorate
a nape of wind with waterbeads;

how all-unseen the spider spins
concentric lacework in the leaves.

So high above tall trees that spear
the sky a bird invisible

is sewing silver threads of song
along the edges of the dawn.

Then, bales of hay on golden slopes,
fourgathered, whispered how

the sap surged upwards, how
the stem and stalk stretched, how

the sudden cut and thrust of scythe
swept all the greensward down.

GIMME THAT OLD-TIME RELIGION
(Surrounded by the flames of Hell, one sufferer confides to another:
"I wouldn't mind only I'm down here for something that isn't a sin
anymore!" — Cartoon)

Once there was a time
when Ireland's spiritual empire
daily spread unchecked throughout
the world and sin came in two sizes
only, and none of your modern stuff
about circumstance and psychology
and the host held in the hand.

Once there was a time
you had to fast from midnight
and have the right intention
and walk with head bowed down
back up the aisle or else
a thunderbolt and brimstone
would destroy you where you knelt.

Once there was a time
our saints and scholars stemmed
the heathen tides of Europe -
Long before the slide began
with upstarts like Copernicus
who took the sun and stuck it
like a thumbtack in the sky.

Once there was a time
that Heaven was a place
where fond-remembered relatives
rubbed elbows with the saints
assured the body would be handed
back intact (as good as new,
in fact) on the Last Day.

Once there was a time
the needle's eye ensured
a better class of blessed,
and Purgatorial fires took pains
with small, but stubborn, stains
and Limbo, although feeble,
had not yet become a dance.

38

And once there was a time
the neon lights of Hell flashed
day and night, while outside
on the steps in cap and braid
a horny devil kept his pitchfork bright
for those who all their lives
had been a trial to decent people.

MY GRANDMOTHER KNEW JESUS

The day I brought from school 'The Messenger'
that pictured out Our Saviour as a Zulu
my grandmother stopped washing, stropped her hands
of suds and held the page at arms' length:
"That's not Jesus".

Innocent of artifice and brimming
soft with childhood grace I asked her why.
"Because — and you should know by now,
whatever 'tis they're teaching ye these days —
Jesus wasn't black".

From Sunday's early Mass she brought me back
a family snap — Mary in her garden,
Joseph planing wood, and Jesus grown
a fine young lad: brown hair, dark eyes,
most definitely Caucasian.

DURABILITY
(in memory of Donal O'Keeffe, Carrowkeal, Crusheen, Co. Clare)

On rainy days my father sat it out
complaining in the kitchen, passing time
in patching up his overalls — So patched
already they, that it was hard to see
how he could find a stretch of gabardine,
a single seam unpitted by his years
of careful stitching. And he'd grumble at the way
things fall apart. One time (he'd say) they'd last.

And once my mother told me (was it just
a bedtime story?) of the mediaeval dancers
who performed a pagan liturgy until
a Pope forbade it. And how he was persuaded
to allow that they continue till their costumes
were worn out. And how by subterfuge
of needles plied in secret they performed
beyond his passing, and even to this day.

I think if I went up and searched our loft
I'd find those overalls still hanging there,
beside the big horsecollar and the rusting scythe
just where he left them on that day he sensed
he'd never need to patch them anymore.
And, though damp and mouldy, they'd be wearable
as yet — Despite all his complaining proved to be
of substance far more durable than he.

Ω

40